The Cricket Quiz Book

CW01424978

The Cricket Quiz Book

by

Chris Coley

Assisted by Bob Nocton

Introduced by

David Gower

EP Publishing Limited

Published by EP Publishing Limited, Bradford Road, East Ardsley, West
Yorkshire, WF3 2JN

ISBN 0 7158 0881 8 (cased)
    0 7158 0851 6 (limp)

British Library Cataloguing in Publication Data

Coley, Chris
    The cricket quiz book.
    1. Cricket — Miscellanea
    I. Title
    796.35'8'076   GV917

    ISBN 0-7158-0851-6

The Cricket Quiz Book
The author would like to stress that all answers were correct at the time of
compilation (1 April 1983). Due to the nature of sport, however, it is possible
that results from future sporting events may affect the accuracy of
information contained in this book.

Acknowledgements
Thanks are due to Geoff Jones for the illustrations and also to the following
for kind permission to reproduce copyright material:
All Sport p.12
Central Press Photos Ltd p.28
Patrick Eagar pp.6 and 40
S & G Press Agency p.15

Printed in Great Britain by
Hazell Watson & Viney Ltd., Aylesbury, Bucks.

Design and Typesetting by
The Word Factory, Rossendale, Lancashire.

Introduction

Cricket is the sort of game which just lends itself to the quiz master's art. There are so many facts and figures to juggle with and well-known personalities to recall, that a quiz book on this popular sport is bound to be a winner.

To give an answer to a traditionally-phrased question is often straightforward, but how about working out the names of a handful of cricketers' surnames from humorous cartoon drawings, or making your way through a square full of letters from jumbled-up counties? Chris Coley has made sure that there's a real variety of questions to cater for your different moods. And, because he covers numerous cricketing topics, it's exciting to see how many answers you can get. If you think you know your cricket, you'll soon find out whether you're right!

David Gower

A famous cricket ground

The photograph was taken at the most famous cricket ground in the world. Answer the following questions about this ground.

1. What is the name of the ground?

. . . .

2. What is the name of the world-famous cricket club that was founded in 1787 and has its headquarters at the ground?

. . . .

3. You are looking towards the Pavilion End but what is the name of the other end?

. . . .

4. The main gates bear the name of which celebrated old England cricketer?

. . . .

5. What is the name of the Members' Room on the ground floor of the pavilion?

. . . .

6. What is the name of the viewing (and drinking) area sited next to the Mound Stand?

. . . .

7. There are squash courts at the ground, and also a court for another sport which is one of the few courts in the country — what is the sport?

. . . .

Please see page 51 for answers

Age

1. Who is the youngest man to have captained England in a Test Match since the World War II?

. . . .

2. Who was the oldest man to play in the county championship in England in 1982?

. . . .

3. Which Sussex and Pakistani cricketer is the youngest man to have scored a double-century in a Test Match?

. . . .

4. Which Kent cricketer took the 1,000th wicket of his first-class career in the 1970–71 season at the age of only 25?

. . . .

5. Which famous Surrey and England opener, whose career spanned the years 1905–1934, scored over a hundred centuries after the age of 40?

. . . .

6. Which Pakistani, a member of a famous cricketing family, in 1959 became the youngest ever Test Match player at the age of 15 years 124 days?

. . . .

7. Which is the 'newest' of the sides in the county championship, having joined the competition in 1920?

. . . .

8. Which former Yorkshire and Somerset all-rounder was recalled to the England Test team in 1976 at the age of 45?

. . . .

9. Which Indian all-rounder broke Ian Botham's record by becoming the youngest player to achieve the Test double of scoring 1,000 runs and taking 100 wickets?

. . . .

10. At the age of 23 he became the youngest Australian bowler to take 100 Test wickets, and at 27 the youngest to take 250 Test wickets. He played for Leicestershire between 1969 and 1976. Who is he?

. . . .

Please see page 51 for answers

An experienced England XI

The team sheet below, with blanks to represent letters of players' surnames, lists an England team picked from those players who have made **50** or more appearances for England and who also played Test cricket in the 1970s. The players' batting positions are not necessarily the ones that they regularly occupied for England. Clues are given in the form of the players' counties at the time of their first caps, and also the years in which they won their first caps.

1. Surrey   1963

_ _ _ _ _ _

2. Yorkshire   1964

_ _ _ _ _ _ _

3. Warwickshire   1966

_ _ _ _ _

4. Kent   1954

_ _ _ _ _ _ _

5. Essex   1968

_ _ _ _ _ _ _ _

6. Somerset   1977

_ _ _ _ _

7. Sussex   1972

_ _ _ _

8. Kent   1967

_ _ _ _ _

9. Yorkshire   1958

_ _ _ _ _ _ _ _ _ _

10. Kent   1966

_ _ _ _ _ _ _ _

11. Surrey   1970

_ _ _ _ _ _

8

Please see page 51 for answers

Anagrams

Unravel the following to find the surnames of cricketers who have all played Test cricket for England since World War II.

1. YEW ILL
A current Northants all-rounder.

. . . .

2. LOW ROME
A Kent opener.

. . . .

3. HOT NUT
A former opening batsman and England captain.

. . . .

4. ROW ONE DUD
A current Kent slow bowler.

. . . .

5. HAT MAST
A former Lancashire seam bowler.

. . . .

6. RAVE AT
A current county captain.

. . . .

7. RED TEX
A former Sussex batsman.

. . . .

8. HE SAY
A Lancashire batsman.

. . . .

9. HER CLEFT
Another current county captain.

. . . .

10. IT MUST
A former Middlesex off-spinner.

. . . .

11. SPARK
A former Sussex wicket-keeper/batsman.

. . . .

12. I SWILL
England's main strike bowler over the last few years.

. . . .

Please see page 51 for answers

Australia

1. Who made the highest score for Australia against England in the 1982–83 series?

....

2. Who took 42 wickets in his first Test series in 1981?

....

3. Which ground was the first to stage 75 Test Matches?

....

4. Who captained Australia in the Cornhill Centenary Test in 1980?

....

5. Which is the 'youngest' Test Match ground in Australia?

....

6. For which English county side did Greg Chappell play?

....

7. What is the highest score by an Australian in Test cricket?

....

8. Which current Australian player is the only man to have scored at least 150 in each innings of a Test Match?

....

9. Who, in 1981, was released by Gloucestershire to play Test cricket for Australia the following day?

....

10. Which Australian state team has never won the Sheffield Shield?

....

11. For which county team did Allan Border play one game?

....

12. Who captained Australia against England in the 1978–79 series?

....

Please see page 51 for answers

Big hitting

1. Who hit 6 sixes in one over against Glamorgan at Swansea in 1968?

....

2. Which Warwickshire player struck 13 sixes in a double-century against Lancashire in 1982?

....

3. Which Yorkshire batsman hit 100 in 37 minutes in a match against Warwickshire in 1977, his second 50 taking just *9 minutes*?

....

4. Which West Indian batsman is the only man to have hit 13 sixes in a single innings on *two* occasions?

....

5. Who made the fastest 100 of the 1982 season, taking just 52 minutes to destroy the Warwickshire attack?

....

6. Which Gloucestershire player struck Denis Breakwell of Somerset for 6 successive sixes in 1979, but not in one over?

....

7. Who hit a century off just 81 balls against England in a Test Match in February 1982?

....

8. Who, in February 1980, hit his maiden Test hundred in a match against the West Indies off just 88 balls?

....

9. Who hit 32 runs off *one* over bowled by Alvin Kallicharan in the Schweppes County Championship in 1982?

....

10. Which cricketer, nicknamed 'the croucher', is renowned for being the greatest hitter of sixes in the history of cricket?

....

11. Which batsman hit 22 off a Bob Willis over to give his team victory in a Benson and Hedges one-day international match in Australia in January 1983?

....

Please see page 52 for answers

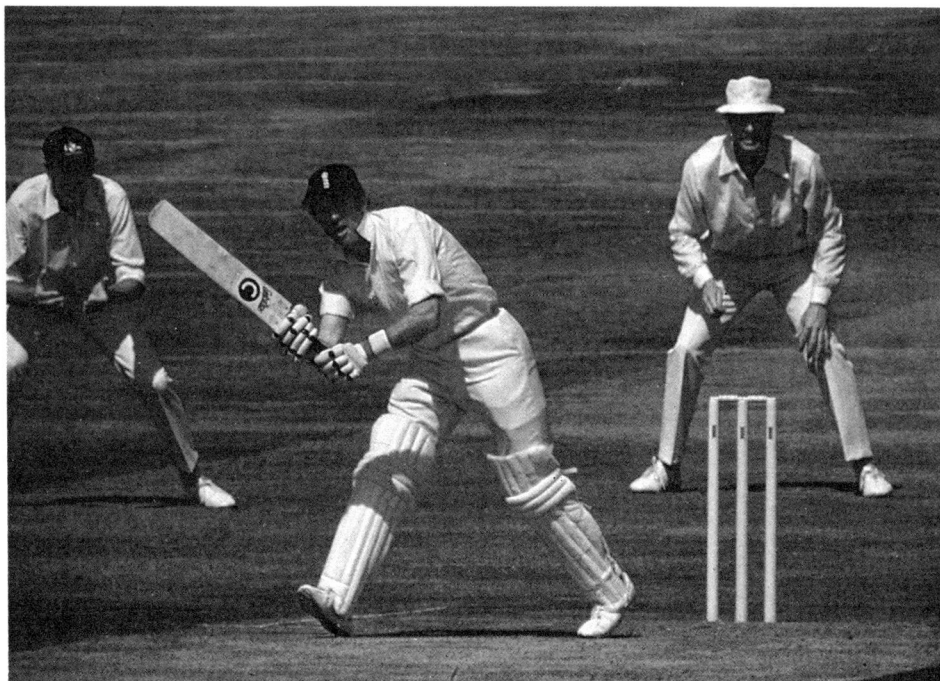

A hundredth century

The picture shows a leading English batsman on his way to scoring his hundredth 100 in first-class cricket and at the same time becoming the first player to achieve this feat in a Test Match.

1. Who is the batsman?

2. On what ground did he achieve this feat?

3. What was the year?

4. Who was the bowler?

5. The batsman also made his highest first-class score on this ground — who were his opponents?

6. What was the actual score?

7. Why was the batsman not selected for the next Test?

8. The batsman made his début for England at Trent Bridge in 1964 in a match against Australia — who was his very first English opening partner?

Please see page 52 for answers

Big scores

1. Who was once run out for 499 in a first-class match?

. . . .

2. Whose score of 365 not out is the highest innings by any player in a Test Match?

. . . .

3. Who was the Englishman whose record of 364 was beaten by the above?

. . . .

4. Which current county cricketer has achieved the feat of scoring a double hundred and a single hundred in the same match on the most number of occasions?

. . . .

5. Which player, later to become an England Test captain, scored 312 not out for M.C.C. Under 25 in Pakistan during the 1966–67 series?

. . . .

6. Who scored 361 runs in *six* first-class innings in April 1982?

. . . .

7. Who was the England opening batsman who scored 310 not out in a match against New Zealand at Leeds in 1965?

. . . .

8. Which Australian batsman scored over 300 in a single innings on *six* occasions in his first-class career?

. . . .

9. Who hit 201 not out in just 120 minutes in a match against Glamorgan at Swansea in 1976?

. . . .

10. Who was the Australian batsman who made scores of 429 and 437 for Victoria in the 1920s?

. . . .

11. Who, in January 1983, broke Viv Richard's record score in a Benson and Hedges World Series one-day international?

. . . .

Please see page 52 for answers

Bowlers

Below is a list of counties and the names of three bowlers associated with each county. Two from every trio are regarded as fast or seam bowlers, but you must select the spin or slow bowler.

1. Derbyshire
Tunnicliffe Miller Oldham

....

2. Essex
Lever Turner Acfield

....

3. Glamorgan
Barwick Lloyd Ontong

....

4. Gloucestershire
Childs Shepherd Bainbridge

....

5. Hampshire
Emery Cowley Jesty

....

6. Kent
Johnson Dilley Jarvis

....

7. Lancashire
Folley Allott Simmons

....

8. Leicestershire
Cook Taylor Parsons

....

9. Middlesex
Hughes Cowans Edmonds

....

10. Northants
Griffiths Willey Mallender

....

11. Notts
Cooper Saxelby Hemmings

....

12. Somerset
Moseley Dredge Marks

....

13. Surrey
Knight Pocock Thomas

....

14. Sussex
Waller Greig Pigott

....

15. Warwickshire
Willis Gifford Small

....

16. Worcestershire
Perryman Inchmore Patel

....

17. Yorkshire
Carrick Sidebottom Stevenson

....

14

Please see page 52 for answers

Photo quiz

This photograph shows Jim Laker in action.

1. Where was the Test Match played in which he took 19 wickets?

2. What was the year?

3. From which end did he take each of these wickets?

4. Who was the only Australian not to be dismissed twice by Laker in the match?

5. Which bowler took the one other wicket?

6. Which two Australians 'bagged a pair' in the match

7. Which two English batsmen made centuries in the match?

8. Which English fielder took five catches in the match?

9. Jim Laker also took 10 wickets in an innings for his county Surrey during this same season — who were Surrey's opponents?

Please see page 53 for answers

Captains

1. Who preceded Bob Willis as captain of England?

....

2. Who, since the Second World War, captained England 41 times?

....

3. Two county captains in 1982 had the same Christian name. Who were they?

....

4. Who captained India against Pakistan in their 1982–83 series?

....

5. Who captained England on the infamous 'body-line' 1932–33 tour?

....

6. Who once declared his county's innings closed after one over to ensure his side reached the final stages of the Benson and Hedges Cup?

....

7. Who is the longest-serving current county captain?

....

8. Who captained the first 'rebel' tour to South Africa?

....

9. Who, on the 1974–75 tour made the highest score by an England captain in a Test Match in Australia?

....

10. Who captained New Zealand in their only Test victory over England in the 1977–78 series?

....

11. Which post-war Test captain only had one eye?

....

16

Please see page 53 for answers

R	A	L	S	E	E	U	S	E	S
N	U	E	H	L	T	D	R	I	S
H	R	E	M	S	E	C	A	E	O
I	I	Y	H	D	H	D	A	S	M
N	S	E	R	G	R	Y	R	C	E
E	H	I	I	W	R	O	I	C	E
X	R	H	A	E	L	E	A	X	R
S	S	X	P	S	O	E	M	T	G
S	L	S	E	R	B	S	E	S	S
R	I	S	R	E	E	R	E	T	M

Beneath you will find a list of cricketers who captained their counties during 1982. The names of their counties are hidden above. Eliminate each player by crossing off the letters in his county team until you are left with just one county in the square. Who captained this county at the end of the season?

1. M. Brearley

2. B. Rose

3. R. Tolchard

4. N. Pocock

5. C. Lloyd

6. K. Fletcher

7. P. Neale

8. R. Knight

9. B. Wood

10. J. Barclay

County badges

Pair up the county badges with the first-class cricket counties that are outlined on the map.

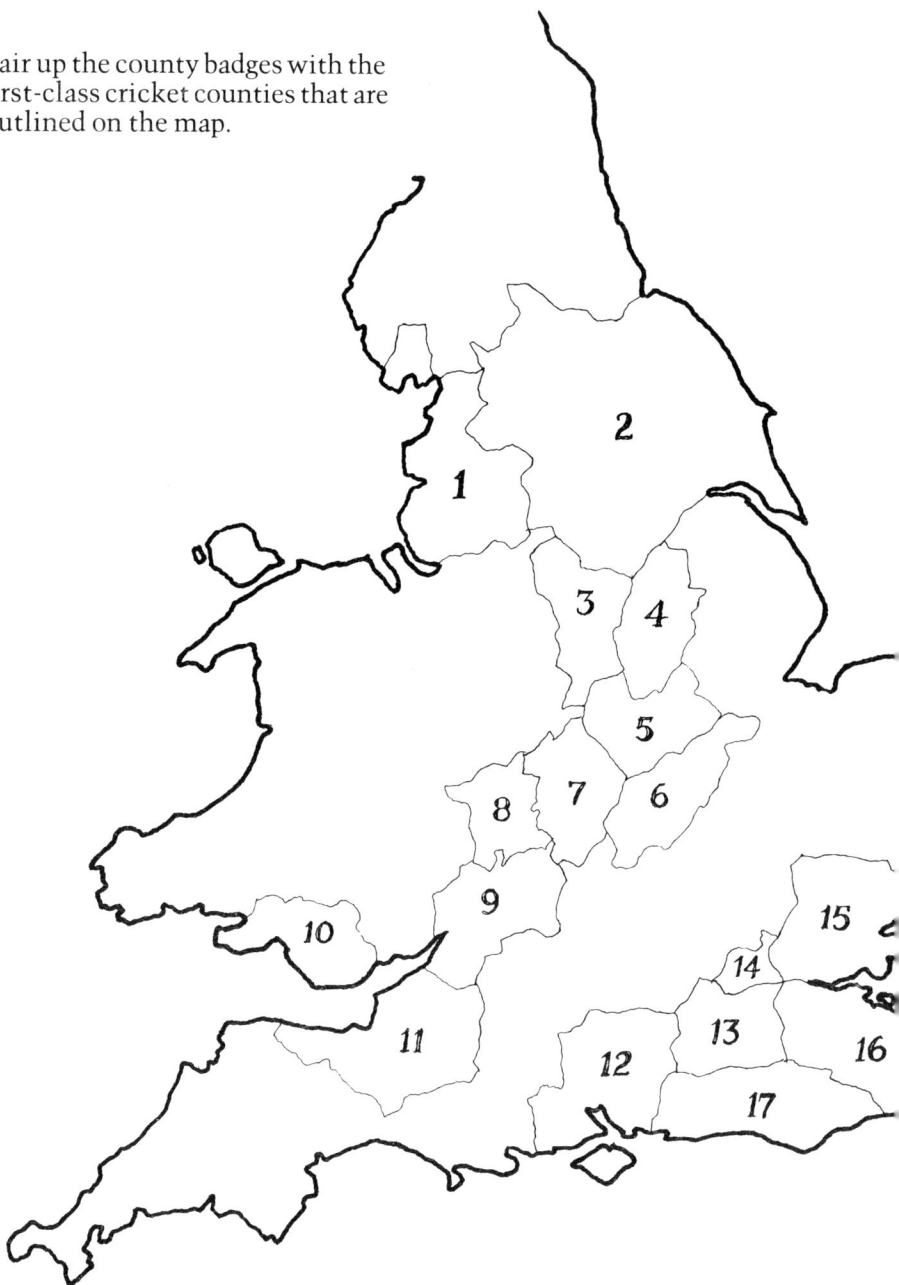

Please see page 53 for answers

A

G

M

B

H

N

C

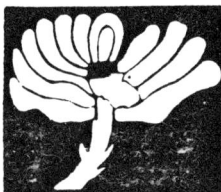

I

O

D

J

P

E

K

Q

F

L

19

County partnerships

On the left is a list of county opening batsmen who have established themselves in the 1980s. On the right is a list of middle order batsmen who have done likewise. Sort the two lists out so that players from the same county are paired together.

1. Geoff Cook	**1.** Peter Roebuck
2. Graham Gooch	**2.** Paul Parker
3. Alan Butcher	**3.** Geoff Humpage
4. Geoff Boycott	**4.** Allan Lamb
5. Peter Denning	**5.** Chris Tavare
6. Denis Amiss	**6.** Clive Radley
7. John Wright	**7.** Keith Fletcher
8. Glenn Turner	**8.** David Turner
9. Bob Woolmer	**9.** Roger Knight
10. Gehan Mendis	**10.** Bill Athey
11. Gordon Greenidge	**11.** Geoff Miller
12. Mike Brearley	**12.** Phil Neale

Please see page 54 for answer.

Cricket and other sports

1. Which former England Test captain won the President's Putter at Rye early in 1983?

. . . .

2. Which current Leicestershire player has played hockey for Rhodesia?

. . . .

3. Who is the current county captain who plays professional soccer for Lincoln City?

. . . .

4. Which current Gloucestershire player was a regular full-back for England at Rugby Union before injuries forced him to retire from the game?

. . . .

5. Which West Indian Test cricketer has played soccer in the World Cup for Antigua?

. . . .

6. Which former Warwickshire and England bowler now breeds racehorses?

. . . .

7. Who played Test cricket for England in 1982 having won Rugby Blues for Cambridge in 1977 and 1978?

. . . .

8. Which current Essex cricketer has fenced for Great Britain in the Olympic Games of 1968 and 1972?

. . . .

9. Who was the last England Test cricketer to also win an international soccer cap for England?

. . . .

10. Dusty Hare, the England Rugby Union full-back, played first-class cricket for which county?

. . . .

Please see page 54 for answers

21

Cryptic illustrations

Below are 6 illustrations with the clues to the cricketers' surnames being found in the drawings. Use your imagination to decipher each well-known Test player.

① *A West Indian fast bowler*

② *A former England captain*

③ *A former England fast bowler*

Please see page 54 for answer.

④ A former England fast bowler

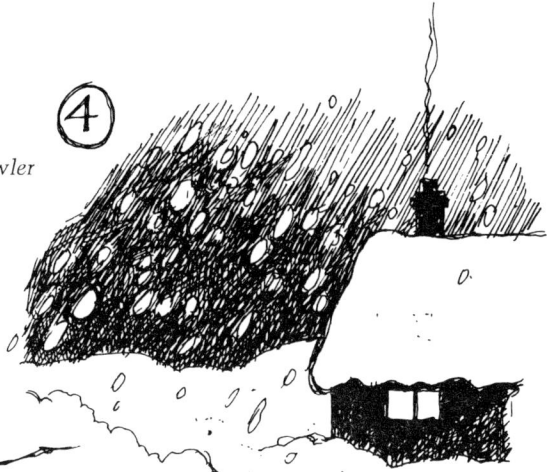

⑤ An Australian wicket-keeper

⑥ A current England all-rounder

FLOUR

Current capped county cricketers

			E						

1. [ ][ ][ ][E]

2. [ ][ ][ ][ ][E]

3. [ ][ ][ ][ ][ ][E]

4. [ ][ ][ ][ ][ ][ ][E]

5. [ ][ ][ ][ ][ ][ ][ ][E]

6. [ ][ ][ ][ ][ ][ ][ ][ ][E]

7. [ ][ ][ ][ ][ ][ ][ ][ ][ ][E]

8. [ ][ ][ ][ ][ ][ ][ ][ ][ ][ ][E]

The missing squares above all need to be filled in with the names of current, capped county cricketers. To make it easier for you each name ends in 'E'.

1. A Notts left arm bowler.

2. A Worcestershire batsman.

3. A Kent batsman.

4. An Essex all-rounder.

5. A Worcestershire seam bowler.

6. A Hampshire batsman.

7. A Gloucestershire all-rounder.

8. A Leicestershire batsman.

Please see page 54 for answer

Débuts

1. Which former Kent and West Indian all-rounder made his début for Gloucestershire in 1982?

. . . .

2. Two Englishmen made their Test débuts against Pakistan in July 1982 at Edgbaston — Eddie Hemmings and which Sussex player?

. . . .

3. Which Australian hit 162 against England on his Test début in November 1982?

. . . .

4. The son of a former England cricketer made his début for Worcestershire in 1982 — who was he?

. . . .

5. Which Australian pace bowler took 16 wickets in the match on his Test début at Lord's in 1972?

. . . .

6. Which England opener made his Test début against Pakistan at Headingley in August 1982?

. . . .

7. Who made his début for Hampshire in 1982 and took 83 first-class wickets?

. . . .

8. Which Australian scored a century on his Test début against England at the Oval in August 1981?

. . . .

9. Which West Indian in the 1971–72 season became the only cricketer to hit centuries in both innings of his Test début?

. . . .

10. Which Surrey bowler, later to become chairman of the Test selectors, took 11 for 145 on his Test début for England against India in 1946?

. . . .

Please see page 54 for answers

England

1. What is the smallest run difference to win an England v. Australia Test Match?

....

2. Which batsman made the highest score in the triangular 1983 Benson and Hedges World Series matches in Australia?

....

3. Who captained England in the Cornhill Centenary Test in 1980?

....

4. At Headingley in 1981, who scored 56, putting on 117 for the eighth wicket with Ian Botham?

....

5. Who took 4 wickets in 5 balls in a Test Match in 1978?

....

6. Which seam bowler has taken over 80 wickets for England, but never more than 4 in an innings?

....

7. For which county did TV broadcaster Jim Laker play when he was a regular member of the England XI?

....

8. Which England wicket-keeper scored over **100** centuries?

....

9. In the 1981 series against Australia, England used 3 wicket-keepers. Taylor and Knott were two. Who was the other?

....

10. On which ground did Geoff Boycott become the leading run-scorer in Test cricket?

....

Please see page 55 for answers

Fielders

1. Which Somerset fielder, uncapped at the start of the season, held most catches during the 1982 season?

. . . .

2. Which current Australian player (excluding Rodney Marsh) has caught out over 100 Test Match batsmen?

. . . .

3. Which current England player has held most catches in Test cricket?

. . . .

4. Who was not retained by Surrey at the end of the 1982 season, having held nearly 600 catches in his first-class career?

. . . .

5. Which other player, who also appeared during the 1982 season, has held over 500 catches in first-class cricket?

. . . .

6. Which West Indian Test player was a leading cover fielder from the mid–'60s to the mid–'70s when he became one of the world's leading slip fielders?

. . . .

7. Who was the post-war South African batsman who was recognised as the greatest cover point of all time?

. . . .

8. Who usually fields in the covers for Leicestershire but often at third slip for England?

. . . .

9. Who during his period as England captain re-introduced the fielding position of silly point in Test Matches?

. . . .

10. Name the West Indian who retired in 1974 having held 109 catches in 93 Test Matches.

. . . .

11. Name the Englishman who retired in 1975 having held 120 catches in 114 Test Matches.

. . . .

12. Which fielder suffered a dislocated shoulder when attempting to arrest a spectator during the 1982–83 Australia v. England series?

. . . .

Please see page 55 for answers

Final ball

The photograph captures the final ball of perhaps the most dramatic Test Match of all time.

1. Which two teams were involved?

. . . .

2. What was the result of the match?

. . . .

3. In which city was the match played?

. . . .

4. In what year?

. . . .

5. Who is the batsman being run out?

. . . .

6. Who is the 'not out' batsman?

. . . .

7. Which fielder had thrown down the wicket?

. . . .

8. Which famous fast bowler had delivered this final ball?

. . . .

Please see page 55 for answers

Great batsmen of the past

County	Career dates	Runs	Highest score	Batsman
1. Gloucestershire	1865–1908	54,896	344	
2. Surrey	1905–1934	61,237	316 n.o.	
3. Glos/Worcs	1948–1971	47,793	258	
4. Hants	1905–1936	55,061	280 n.o.	
5. Kent	1950–1976	42,719	307	
6. Gloucestershire	1920–1951	50,493	336 n.o.	
7. Middlesex	1936–1964	38,942	300	
8. Yorkshire	1934–1960	40,140	364	
9. Kent	1906–1938	58,969	305 n.o.	
10. Yorkshire	1919–1945	50,135	313	
11. Surrey	1956–1978	39,790	310 n.o.	
12. Warwickshire	1951–1975	39,832	204	

Above you will find the career details of 12 of England's greatest batsmen from the past. The 12 are listed in random order below.
Pair them up with their correct records.

Philip Mead	Len Hutton
Wally Hammond	Jack Hobbs
John Edrich	Colin Cowdrey
Frank Woolley	Herbert Sutcliffe
W. G. Grace	Tom Graveney
Mike Smith	Denis Compton

Please see page 55 for answers

Hampshire/Sussex/Kent

1. On which of these counties' grounds is there a tree within the boundary?

. . . .

2. Which Hampshire player was summoned to join the England party in Australia over Christmas 1982?

. . . .

3. Which current Kent cricketer captained the Australian U.19 team on a tour to Pakistan in the 1980–81 series and later in 1981 played for England Young Cricketers?

. . . .

4. Who was the Sussex player who, as a substitute, distinguished himself by brilliantly catching Greg Chappell in the fourth Test at Melbourne in December 1982?

. . . .

5. Which Hampshire bowler took 134 wickets in 1982, the highest number of wickets since the days of uncovered pitches?

. . . .

6. Which Sussex cricketer took a wicket in his first over in Test cricket in July 1982?

. . . .

7. Which former Sussex and England cricketer is Bishop of Liverpool?

. . . .

8. Which Kent and England player, better known for his batting prowess, had the remarkable figures of 6 for 9 in a John Player League game against Derbyshire in 1979?

. . . .

9. Which Kent bowler took 100 wickets in his début season in 1963 and so became the youngest player ever to achieve this feat?

. . . .

10. Which Sussex player, in a Test Match early in 1983, scored a century and took 11 wickets in the same match?

. . . .

Please see page 56 for answers

India/Pakistan

1. Who, in a Test in 1982, became the first Pakistani to score a double-century at Lord's?

. . . .

2. Who, having played in 87 consecutive Tests, was omitted from the Indian team to tour the West Indies in early 1983?

. . . .

3. Which Pakistan opener took 9 hours 17 minutes to score 100 against England in 1978?

. . . .

4. With whom did this same opener put on a record 451 for the third wicket in a match against India in January 1983?

. . . .

5. Which four brothers have *all* appeared in Test Matches for Pakistan since the Second World War?

. . . .

6. Which fielder in 1977 held *seven* catches on his India début?

. . . .

7. Who, in 1982, hit 100 on his Test début for Pakistan having hit 100 in each innings on his first-class début in 1980?

. . . .

8. Which father and son have captained India on tours to England?

. . . .

9. Which player, though not recognised as a front line bowler, dismissed Randall, Lamb and Gower within *six* balls in a Test Match at Lord's in 1982?

. . . .

10. Which father and son have both scored centuries on their Test débuts for India?

. . . .

Please see page 56 for answers

Initials

The initials and surnames of 12 famous post-war English cricketers have been totally mixed up here. Find the cricketer's surname to go with his initials.

1. P.B.H. Cowdrey . . . .

7. F.S. Edrich . . . .

2. R.G.D. Underwood . . . .

8. A.P.E. Willis . . . .

3. J.H. Trueman . . . .

9. M.C. Dexter . . . .

4. D.C.S. Smith . . . .

10. A.V. Randall . . . .

5. D.W. May . . . .

11. E.R. Compton . . . .

6. D.L. Bedser . . . .

12. M.J.K. Knott . . . .

Please see page 56 for answers

Left-handers (batsmen)

Listed below are the names of well-known batsmen. In each case which of the three cricketers is, or was, left-handed?

1. Gordon Greenidge
Clive Lloyd
Viv Richards

. . . .

2. Alan Butcher
Roland Butcher
Basil Butcher

. . . .

3. Ian Botham
Derek Randall
David Gower

. . . .

4. Bobby Simpson
Neil Harvey
Keith Miller

. . . .

5. Alvin Kallicharran
Sunil Gavaskar
Zaheer Abbas

. . . .

6. Colin Cowdrey
Geoff Boycott
John Edrich

. . . .

7. Gary Sobers
Rohan Kanhai
Frank Worrell

. . . .

8. Greg Chappell
Kim Hughes
Allan Border

. . . .

9. Glenn Turner
John Wright
Geoff Howarth

. . . .

10. Brian Rose
Peter Roebuck
Vic Marks

. . . .

Please see page 56 for answers

Left-handers (bowlers)

Which of the following bowlers is, or was, left-handed?

1. Geoff Miller
Phil Edmonds
Eddie Hemmings

. . . .

2. Mike Hendrick
Robin Jackman
Malcolm Nash

. . . .

3. Chris Old
John Lever
John Snow

. . . .

4. Derek Underwood
Ray Illingworth
John Mortimore

. . . .

5. David Allen
Fred Titmus
Norman Gifford

. . . .

6. Madan Lal
Kapil Dev
Bishen Bedi

. . . .

7. Pat Pocock
Vic Marks
Nick Cook

. . . .

8. Dilip Doshi
Imran Khan
Abdul Qadir

. . . .

9. Peter Loader
Tony Lock
Jim Laker

. . . .

10. Wes Hall
Charlie Griffith
Gary Sobers

. . . .

Please see page 57 for answers

New Zealand

1. Who captained New Zealand in the 1983 Triangular One-day series against England and Australia?

. . . .

2. Who were the two New Zealand Test players who played county cricket for Worcestershire in the 1970s?

. . . .

3. New Zealand's premier domestic cricket competition is the Shell Trophy, but by what name was it previously called?

. . . .

4. Who hit 181 for New Zealand in a match against Australia in March 1982?

. . . .

5. Who, in the 1978 England v. New Zealand series, hit the fastest recorded ever 50 and also conceded the most runs ever off his cleven overs?

. . . .

6. Which New Zealander hit *seven* first-class centuries in the 1982 Schweppes County Championships?

. . . .

7. Who has scored the most runs for New Zealand in a Test career?

. . . .

8. Who took a hat-trick for New Zealand in a Test Match at Lahore in 1976–77?

. . . .

9. Which current New Zealand bowler was once very nearly fatally injured when struck by a ball from John Lever?

. . . .

10. Which New Zealand tourist in 1978 took a wicket against England in his first over in Test cricket?

. . . .

Please see page 57 for answers

Newcomers

Below is a list of cricketers who have recently been trying to establish themselves in first-class cricket. For which county does each play?
N.B. There is one player from each county.

1. D.G. Aslett

....

2. S.J. Malone

....

3. I. Folley

....

4. A.M. Green

....

5. A.W. Lilley

....

6. S.N. Hartley

....

7. M.A. Fell

....

8. H. Morris

....

9. N.A. Felton

....

10. K.S. Mackintosh

....

11. M.J. Weston

....

12. A.J. Wright

....

13. Asif Din

....

14. D.J. Capel

....

15. B.J.M. Maher

....

16. R.A. Cobb

....

17. K.P. Tomlins

....

Please see page 57 for answers

Northants/Notts/Derby/ Leicestershire/Warwickshire

1. Which of these counties share their county ground with a Football League soccer club?

. . . .

2. Which Leicestershire player was vice-captain of England on their 1982–83 tour of Australia?

. . . .

3. Which Warwickshire batsman hit 254 against Lancashire in 1982, the highest first-class score by an Englishman in the season?

. . . .

4. Which Derbyshire cricketer made eight centuries for his county in 1982?

. . . .

5. Which Notts player scored 95 in a Test Match for England in 1983 after being sent in as nightwatchman?

. . . .

6. Which cricket manager made history in 1982 by being allowed to bowl as a substitute when one of his players was summoned to join the England Test squad?

. . . .

7. Who scored *seven* centuries for Leicestershire in his benefit season in 1982?

. . . .

8. Which former Northants and England fast bowler commentated on Channel 9 on the 1982–83 Australia v. England Test series?

. . . .

9. Who was the Notts No. 11 who managed to score just *three* runs in his nine first-class innings during 1982?

. . . .

10. Which of the above counties won a one-day trophy at Lord's in 1981 by tieing both the final and previously the semi-final?

. . . .

Please see page 57 for answers

37

One-day cricket

1. Who scored 198 not out in a Benson and Hedges match in 1982?

....

2. Which side dismissed Leicestershire for only 56 (including 15 wides) in a Benson and Hedges match in 1982?

....

3. On which ground is the Tilcon Trophy played?

....

4. Which individual scored a record 146 in the 1965 Gillette Cup final?

....

5. Which country won the International Cricket Conference Trophy Final for non-Test Match playing countries at Leicester in 1982?

....

6. Somerset beat Notts by 9 wickets in the 1982 Benson and Hedges Cup final. Which player won the Gold Award in the final?

....

7. Surrey beat Warwickshire by 9 wickets in the 1982 Nat. West Trophy Final. Which player won the Man of the Match Award in the final?

....

8. Which county won the first Lambert and Butler Floodlit competition in 1981?

....

9. Which is the *only* county not to have appeared in any one-day final at Lord's?

....

10. Which county won three successive Gillette Cup finals in 1970, 1971 and 1972?

....

11. Who holds the records for the highest individual scores in both the Gillette Cup and the John Player League?

....

12. Which *two* countries did England meet in a triangular series of one-day matches during the 1982–83 series?

....

Please see page 58 for answers

Overseas cricketers

The following overseas cricketers all made their mark with their countries in 1982. On the left are the names of 12 cricketers and on the right a list of 11 counties. Match the cricketers with their counties until you are left with one name. For which county did he play?

1. Colin Croft	**A.** Derbyshire
2. Javed Miandad	**B.** Kent
3. Sylvester Clarke	**C.** Gloucestershire
4. Norbert Phillip	**D.** Middlesex
5. Anton Ferreira	**E.** Northants
6. Andy Roberts	**F.** Glamorgan
7. Asif Iqbal	**G.** Essex
8. Garth Le Roux	**H.** Lancashire
9. Franklyn Stephenson	**I.** Surrey
10. John Wright	**J.** Sussex
11. Kapil Dev	**K.** Warwickshire
12. Wayne Daniel	

Please see page 58 for answers

Photo quiz

The photograph shows a group of England cricketers leaving an airport on 27 February 1981 when a Test Match against the West Indies was called off at short notice. Answer the following questions relating to the photograph.

1. On which island is the airport?

2. Who is the player at the centre of the controversy who had been served with a deportation order?

3. The player had recently joined the party as a replacement for which injured player?

4. Who was the English manager who was very much involved in the affair?

5. Who was the English assistant manager/coach who tragically died during the tour?

6. Who are the two players in the photograph on either side of the cricketer who was ordered to be deported?

Please see page 58 for answers

South Africa

1. Who captained the South African XI against the touring West Indians in 1983?

. . . .

2. Which *two* England Test cricketers are currently playing South African first-class cricket for Western Province?

. . . .

3. Which South African hit 325 in a day in the Sheffield Shield Competition in Australia?

. . . .

4. Which South African born cricketer scored a century on his Australian Test début in 1982?

. . . .

5. What is the name of South Africa's premier domestic competition?

. . . .

6. Which South African hit *six* successive first-class centuries in the 1970–71 domestic season?

. . . .

7. Which member of England's 1982–83 touring party to Australia has captained Eastern Province?

. . . .

8. Who was the only uncapped player in the original party on England's rebel tour to South Africa in 1982?

. . . .

9. Which South African took a hat-trick in a Test Match at Lord's in 1960 and never played Test cricket again?

. . . .

10. Who captained South Africa in their last official Test series (1969–70)?

. . . .

Surrey/Middlesex/Essex

1. Which former Essex player managed the England tour to Australia in the 1982–83 series?

. . . .

2. Who captained England on their tour of India during 1981–82 but was dropped by England for the home series in the summer of 1982?

. . . .

3. What particular landmark is associated with the Surrey county ground?

. . . .

4. Which Essex bowler took a wicket with the first ball of the 1981 English season?

. . . .

5. Who played a first-class game for Middlesex in 1982 having begun his first-class career in 1949?

. . . .

6. Which Essex batsman bagged a pair on his England Test début in 1975?

. . . .

7. On which ground did Mike Brearley play his final first-class match?

. . . .

8. Which former Surrey batsman holds the record for scoring 197 first-class centuries in his career?

. . . .

9. Who topped both the batting and bowling averages for Middlesex in 1982?

. . . .

10. Which Surrey batsman was at the non-striking end when both Geoff Boycott and John Edrich each scored their 100th century in 1977?

. . . .

Please see page 58 for answer

The first

1. Who, with a score of 115 at Perth, hit England's first Test century of their 1982–83 tour to Australia?

. . . .

2. Who helped Eddie Hemmings put on 112 for England's tenth wicket against South Australia in November 1982, the first time for nearly 80 years that an England pair had made a three figure score for the last wicket in Australia?

. . . .

3. Which New Zealander, in May 1982, became the first player to reach the milestone of 6,000 runs in the John Player League?

. . . .

4. Who was dismissed off the first ball in the first innings of England's first match against Queensland on their 1982–83 tour of Australia?

. . . .

5. Which Worcestershire cricketer in 1982 became the first man to score a century and take four wickets in the same John Player League match?

. . . .

6. Which was the first minor county to reach the quarter-finals of the Gillette Cup?

. . . .

7. Which Lancashire cricketer in 1980 became the first player to receive a benefit of over £100,000?

. . . .

8. Which country competed in its first official Test Match in February 1982?

. . . .

9. Which southern county won the first two Gillette Cups in 1963 and 1964?

. . . .

10. Which opener, in December 1982, became the first player from Pakistan to score over 1,000 Test runs in a calendar year?

. . . .

Please see page 59 for answers

The last

1. Who was the last Australian to be dismissed — caught Miller off Botham — in Australia's second innings of the memorable Fourth Test at Melbourne in December 1982, to give England victory by just three runs?

....

2. Which was the last first-class county to lose in a three-day game to Cambridge University?

....

3. Which West Indian spinner, later to play for Warwickshire, was the last player from that country to take a Test Match hat-trick?

....

4. Who was the last Englishman to take a hat-trick in a Test Match?

....

5. Which Pakistani fast bowler, who plays for Northants, was the last man to take *nine* wickets in a Test innings?

....

6. Which county won the last Gillette Cup competition in 1980?

....

7. Who was the last Oxford/Cambridge undergraduate to be selected for England while at university?

....

8. Which Lancashire batsman, at the Oval in 1973, was the last Englishman to score a century on his Test début?

....

9. Who was South Africa's last man when they played their last official Test Match against Australia in 1970?

....

10. Which famous Australian batsman was bowled by Eric Hollies for 0 in his last test innings at the Oval in 1948?

....

Please see page 59 for answer

...the only...

1. What is the name of the Pakistani who is the only man to have hit a century in both innings of a match on *eight* occasions?

. . . .

2. Which is the only first-class county to boast a whole team of 'home-grown' players?

. . . .

3. Which wicket-keeper, in November 1982, became the only man to reach the milestone of 300 Test catches?

. . . .

4. Which Australian state side is the only team to have scored over 1,000 runs in one innings?

. . . .

5. Which Kent batsman in 1938 became the only player to hit a double-century in both innings of the same match?

. . . .

6. Which is the only team to have won the National Village Championship on three occasions?

. . . .

7. Which South Africa and Gloucestershire all-rounder in the 1970s became the only cricketer to score a century and take a hat-trick in the same match on two separate occasions?

. . . .

8. Which famous England batsman, who later captained the team, in 1951 became the only man to have been given out 'obstructing the field' in a Test?

. . . .

9. Who, in a Benson and Hedges match against the Combined Universities in 1982, became the only wicket-keeper to take *eight* catches in a one-day match?

. . . .

10. Which Kent bowler in 1928 became the only player to take over 300 wickets in an English season?

. . . .

*lease see page 59 for answers   45

West Indies

1. Name either of the young spin bowlers who bowled West India to victory over England in 1950.

. . . .

2. Name the famous batsmen for the West Indies known as the 'three Ws'.

. . . .

3. Which batsman has scored the most Test runs for the West Indies?

. . . .

4. Which bowler has taken most wickets for the West Indies?

. . . .

5. Who captained the 'rebel' West Indies team in South Africa in the 1982–83 series?

. . . .

6. Who took the most wickets in the 1980 Test series against England?

. . . .

7. Which West Indian scored 291 in a Test Match in 1976 at the Oval?

. . . .

8. Which West Indian opening bowler played for Worcestershire throughout the 1970s?

. . . .

9. Who has scored the most runs in Test cricket, without scoring an individual century?

. . . .

10. In what year did the West Indies play their first Test Match?

. . . .

11. Which West Indian scored his maiden century batting at No. 10 on the 1980 tour of England?

. . . .

12. Which West Indian opening batsman, in terms of balls received, has hit the fastest century in Test cricket?

. . . .

Please see page 59 for answer

Wicket-keepers

1. Who, early in 1983, established a world record 28 dismissals in one Test series?

. . . .

2. Which county wicket-keeper in 1982 had 74 victims in his first full season?

. . . .

3. Which wicket-keeper retired from English first-class cricket at the end of the 1982 season having caught out 622 and stumped 84 batsmen?

. . . .

4. Which current Test wicket-keeper has a shaven head?

. . . .

5. The last two regular West Indian Test wicket-keepers have shared which surname?

. . . .

6. Which England wicket keeper currently plays for Middlesex, having started his first-class career with Kent?

. . . .

7. Which current county wicket-keeper, who has toured with England, was born in Cornwall?

. . . .

8. Which 17 year old missed an 'A' level examination in 1981 to make his first-class début for Gloucestershire?

. . . .

9. Which wicket-keeper made a century in the Melbourne Centenary Test in 1977?

. . . .

10. Which current county wicket-keeper is the son of a former England wicket-keeper?

. . . .

lease see page 60 for answers   47

Worcestershire/Gloucestershire/ Somerset/Glamorgan

1. Which Worcestershire player scored 311 not out in a match against Warwickshire in May 1982?

. . . .

2. Which Gloucestershire batsman hit his 100th first-class century in a Test Match in December 1982?

. . . .

3. Which of the above counties has a county ground that is regularly flooded in winter and is overlooked by a cathedral?

. . . .

4. Which Glamorgan player topped 1,000 runs in a season for the 22nd time in 1982?

. . . .

5. Who was the former Gloucestershire player (and later administrator) who took over as Secretary of Somerset for 1983?

. . . .

6. Which Glamorgan bowler has the dubious distinction of having been hit for both 36 and 34 in a 6-ball over?

. . . .

7. Which uncapped Somerset player hit 100 in each innings against Northants in 1982?

. . . .

8. Which former Worcestershire player's selection for the M.C.C. caused a projected tour to South Africa to be cancelled?

. . . .

9. Which current Test umpire has a son, who made his first-class début for Somerset at the age of 17 years in 1982?

. . . .

10. Which Worcestershire player, who left the county in 1982, after 25 years as a player, was Assistant Manager of the England touring party to Australia during the 1982–83 series?

. . . .

48

Please see page 60 for answer

Yorkshire/Lancashire

1. Yorkshire and Lancashire traditionally play each other to decide the Battle of the . . .?

. . . .

2. Which Yorkshireman has won the most English test caps?

. . . .

3. Who was the only player from one of these counties to go on the 1982–83 England tour to Australia?

. . . .

4. Which Lancashire player has captained the West Indies on the most number of occasions?

. . . .

5. Which Yorkshireman, batting at No. 11, scored 115 not out in a county match against Warwickshire in 1982?

. . . .

6. Which trophy did Lancashire win in 1970, 1971 and 1972?

. . . .

7. Who began the 1982 season as captain of Yorkshire but was later to be replaced by Ray Illingworth?

. . . .

8. Which Lancashire player fractured his leg while taking a run in a match at Lord's in 1982?

. . . .

9. Which Yorkshireman captained England when his team regained the Ashes in 1953?

. . . .

10. Which Lancashire bowler bowled 13 consecutive maiden overs against Gloucestershire in 1980?

. . . .

Please see page 60 for answers

A famous cricket ground

1. Lord's
2. M.C.C.
3. Nursery End
4. Grace Gates
5. Long Room
6. The Tavern
7. Real Tennis

Age

1. Ian Botham
2. Ray Illingworth
3. Javed Miandad
4. Derek Underwood
5. Jack Hobbs
6. Mushtaq Mohammad
7. Glamorgan
8. Brian Close
9. Kapil Dev
10. Graham McKenzie

An experienced England XI

1. John Edrich
2. Geoff Boycott
3. Denis Amiss
4. Colin Cowdrey
5. Keith Fletcher
6. Ian Botham
7. Tony Greig
8. Alan Knott
9. Ray Illingworth
10. Derek Underwood
11. Bob Willis

Anagrams

1. (Peter) Willey
2. (Bob) Woolmer
3. (Len) Hutton
4. (Derek) Underwood
5. (Brian) Statham
6. (Chris) Tavare
7. (Ted) Dexter
8. (Frank) Hayes
9. (Keith) Fletcher
10. (Fred) Titmus
11. (Jim) Parks
12. (Bob) Willis

Australia

1. Kepler Wessels
2. Terry Alderman
3. Melbourne
4. Greg Chappell
5. Perth
6. Somerset
7. 334 by Don Bradman

8. Allan Border
9. Mike Whitney
10. Queensland
11. Gloucestershire
12. Graham Yallop

Big hitting

1. Garfield Sobers
2. Geoff Humpage
3. Chris Old
4. Gordon Greenidge
5. Ian Botham
6. Mike Procter
7. Kapil Dev
8. Richard Hadlee
9. Paul Parker
10. Gilbert Jessop
11. David Hookes

A hundredth century

1. Geoff Boycott
2. Headingley
3. 1977
4. Greg Chappell
5. India
6. 246 not out
7. As a disciplinary measure for his slow scoring
8. Fred Titmus

Big scores

1. Hanif Mohammad
2. Garfield Sobers
3. Len Hutton
4. Zaheer Abbas
5. Mike Brearley
6. Derek Pringle
7. John Edrich
8. Don Bradman
9. Clive Lloyd
10. Bill Ponsford
11. David Gower

Bowlers

1. Miller
2. Acfield
3. Lloyd
4. Childs
5. Cowley
6. Johnson
7. Simmons
8. Cook
9. Edmonds
10. Willey
11. Hemmings
12. Marks
13. Pocock
14. Waller
15. Gifford
16. Patel
17. Carrick

Photo Quiz

1. Old Trafford
2. 1956
3. Stretford End
4. Jim Burke
5. Tony Lock
6. Neil Harvey and Ken Mackay
7. Peter Richardson and Rev. David Sheppard
8. Alan Oakman
9. Again against the Australians

Captains

1. Keith Fletcher
2. Peter May
3. Roger Knight and Roger Tolchard
4. Sunil Gavaskar
5. Douglas Jardine
6. Brian Rose
7. Keith Fletcher
8. Graham Gooch
9. Mike Denness
10. Mark Burgess
11. The Nawab of Pataudi Junior

County captains

1. Middlesex
2. Somerset
3. Leicestershire
4. Hampshire
5. Lancashire
6. Essex
7. Worcestershire
8. Surrey
9. Derbyshire
10. Sussex
   The remaining county is Glamorgan — the team was captained by Barry Lloyd

County badges

1.	H	Lancashire
2.	I	Yorkshire
3.	L	Derbyshire
4.	G	Nottinghamshire
5.	E	Leicestershire
6.	P	Northamptonshire
7.	C	Warwickshire
8.	Q	Worcestershire
9.	M	Gloucestershire
10.	O	Glamorgan
11.	J	Somerset
12.	K	Hampshire
13.	F	Surrey
14.	B	Middlesex
15.	A	Essex
16.	D	Kent
17.	N	Sussex

County partnerships

1. Geoff Cook and Allan Lamb
2. Graham Gooch and Keith Fletcher
3. Alan Butcher and Roger Knight
4. Geoff Boycott and Bill Athey
5. Peter Denning and Peter Roebuck
6. Denis Amiss and Geoff Humpage
7. John Wright and Geoff Miller
8. Glenn Turner and Phil Neale
9. Bob Woolmer and Chris Tavare
10. Gehan Mendis and Paul Parker
11. Gordon Greenidge and David Turner
12. Mike Brearley and Clive Radley

Cricket and other sports

1. Ted Dexter
2. Brian Davison
3. Phil Neale
4. Alastair Hignell
5. Viv Richards
6. David Brown
7. Ian Greig
8. David Acfield
9. Arthur Milton
10. Nottinghamshire

Cryptic illustrations

1. (Colin) Croft
2. (Keith) Fletcher
3. (Chris) Old
4. (John) Snow
5. (Rod) Marsh
6. (Geoff) Miller

Current capped county cricketers

1. Mike Bore
2. Phil Neale
3. Chris Tavare
4. Derek Pringle
5. John Inchmore
6. Gordon Greenidge
7. Philip Bainbridge
8. Chris Balderstone

Débuts

1. John Shepherd
2. Ian Greig
3. Kepler Wessels
4. Damien D'Oliviera
5. Bob Massie
6. Graeme Fowler
7. Kevin Emery

8. Dirk Wellham
9. Lawrence Rowe
10. Alec Bedser

England

1. 3 runs
2. David Gower
3. Ian Botham
4. Graham Dilley
5. Chris Old
6. Mike Hendrick
7. Surrey
8. Les Ames
9. Paul Downton
10. Delhi

Fielders

1. Jeremy Lloyds
2. Greg Chappell
3. Ian Botham
4. Graham Roope
5. Keith Fletcher
6. Clive Lloyd
7. Colin Bland
8. David Gower
9. Tony Greig
10. Garfield Sobers
11. Colin Cowdrey
12. Terry Alderman

Final ball

1. West Indies and Australia
2. A tie
3. Brisbane
4. 1960
5. Ian Meckiff
6. Lindsay Kline
7. Joe Solomon
8. Wes Hall

Great batsmen of the past

1. W.G. Grace
2. Jack Hobbs
3. Tom Graveney
4. Philip Mead
5. Colin Cowdrey
6. Wally Hammond
7. Denis Compton
8. Len Hutton
9. Frank Woolley
10. Herbert Sutcliffe
11. John Edrich
12. Mike Smith

Hampshire/ Sussex/Kent

1. Kent (St. Lawrence Ground, Canterbury)
2. Trevor Jesty
3. Laurie Potter
4. Ian Gould
5. Malcolm Marshall
6. Ian Greig
7. David Sheppard
8. Bob Woolmer
9. Derek Underwood
10. Imran Khan

Initials

1. P.H.B. May
2. R.G.D. Willis
3. J.H. Edrich
4. D.C.S. Compton
5. D.W. Randall
6. D.L. Underwood
7. F.S. Trueman
8. A.P.E. Knott
9. M.C. Cowdrey
10. A.V. Bedser
11. E.R. Dexter
12. M.J.K. Smith

India/Pakistan

1. Mohsin Khan
2. Gundappa Vishwanath
3. Mudassar Nazar
4. Javed Miandad
5. Hanif, Wazir, Mushtaq and Sadiq Mohammad
6. Yajurvindra Singh
7. Salim Malik
8. The Pataudis
9. Mudassar Nazar
10. The Amarnaths

Left-handers (batsmen)

1. Clive Lloyd
2. Alan Butcher
3. David Gower
4. Neil Harvey
5. Alvin Kallicharran
6. John Edrich
7. Gary Sobers
8. Allan Border
9. John Wright
10. Brian Rose

Left-handers (bowlers)

1. Phil Edmonds
2. Malcolm Nash
3. John Lever
4. Derek Underwood
5. Norman Gifford
6. Bishen Bedi
7. Nick Cook
8. Dilip Doshi
9. Tony Lock
10. Gary Sobers

New Zealand

1. Geoff Howarth
2. Glenn Turner and John Parker
3. The Plunkett Shield
4. Bruce Edgar
5. Lance Cairns
6. John Wright
7. Bevan Congdon
8. Peter Petherick
9. Ewan Chatfield
10. Brendan Bracewell

Newcomers

1. Kent
2. Hampshire
3. Lancashire
4. Sussex
5. Essex
6. Yorkshire
7. Nottinghamshire
8. Glamorgan
9. Somerset
10. Surrey
11. Worcestershire
12. Gloucestershire
13. Warwickshire
14. Northamptonshire
15. Derbyshire
16. Leicestershire
17. Middlesex

Northants/Notts/ Derby/ Leicestershire/ Warwickshire

1. Northants
2. David Gower
3. Geoff Humpage
4. Peter Kirsten
5. Eddie Hemmings
6. David Brown
7. Brian Davison
8. Frank Tyson
9. Peter Such
10. Derbyshire

One-day cricket

1. Graham Gooch
2. Minor Counties
3. Harrogate
4. Geoff Boycott
5. Zimbabwe
6. Vic Marks
7. David Thomas
8. Lancashire
9. Hampshire
10. Lancashire
11. Gordon Greenidge
12. Australia/New Zealand

Overseas cricketers

1. Colin Croft — Lancashire
2. Javed Miandad — Glamorgan
3. Sylvester Clarke — Surrey
4. Norbert Phillip — Essex
5. Anton Ferreira — Warwickshire
7. Asif Iqbal — Kent
8. Garth Le Roux — Sussex
9. Franklyn Stephenson — Gloucestershire
10. John Wright — Derbyshire
11. Kapil Dev — Northants
12. Wayne Daniel — Middlesex
    The missing cricketer is Andy Roberts who played for Leicestershire

Photo quiz

1. Guyana
2. Robin Jackman
3. Bob Willis
4. Alan Smith
5. Ken Barrington
6. David Gower and Mike Gatting

South Africa

1. Peter Kirsten
2. Graham Gooch and John Emburey
3. Barry Richards
4. Kepler Wessels
5. The Currie Cup
6. Mike Procter
7. Geoff Cook
8. Les Taylor
9. Geoff Griffin
10. Ali Bacher

Surrey/Middlesex/ Essex

1. Doug Insole
2. Keith Fletcher
3. A gasometer

4. John Lever
5. Fred Titmus
6. Graham Gooch
7. Worcester
8. Jack Hobbs
9. Mike Gatting
10. Graham Roope

The first

1. Derek Randall
2. Robin Jackman
3. Glenn Turner
4. Geoff Cook
5. Dipak Patel
6. Hertfordshire in 1976
7. Jack Simmons
8. Sri Lanka
9. Sussex
10. Mohsin Khan

The last

1. Jeff Thomson
2. Lancashire in 1982
3. Lance Gibbs
4. Peter Loader
5. Sarfraz Nawaz v. Australia in the 1978–79 series
6. Middlesex
7. Derek Pringle
8. Frank Hayes
9. A.J. Traicos
10. Don Bradman

... the only ...

1. Zaheer Abbas
2. Yorkshire
3. Rod Marsh
4. Victoria
5. Arthur Fagg
6. Troon
7. Mike Procter
8. Len Hutton
9. Derek Taylor
10. Tich Freeman

West Indies

1. Sonny Ramadhin and Alf Valentine
2. Clyde Walcott, Everton Weekes and Frank Worrell
3. Gary Sobers
4. Lance Gibbs
5. Lawrence Rowe
6. Joel Garner
7. Viv Richards
8. Vanburn Holder
9. D.L. Murray
10. 1928
11. Joel Garner
12. Roy Fredericks

Wicket-keepers

1. Rod Marsh
2. David East
3. Derek Taylor
4. S.M.H. Kirmani
5. Murray (Derek and David)
6. Paul Downton
7. Jack Richards
8. Robert Russell
9. Rod Marsh
10. Bobby Parks

Worcestershire/ Gloucestershire/ Somerset/ Glamorgan

1. Glenn Turner
2. Zaheer Abbas
3. Worcester
4. Alan Jones
5. Tony Brown
6. Malcolm Nash
7. Jeremy Lloyds
8. Basil D'Oliviera
9. Ken Palmer
10. Norman Gifford

Yorkshire/ Lancashire

1. Roses
2. Geoff Boycott
3. Graeme Fowler
4. Clive Lloyd
5. Graham Stevenson
6. Gillette Cup
7. Chris Old
8. Frank Hayes
9. Len Hutton
10. David Hughes

Notes

Notes

Notes

Notes